How to Escape an Abusive Relationship

By

Dottie Randazzo

How to Escape an Abusive Relationship

by

Dottie Randazzo

Published by:

Creative Dreaming

6433 Topanga Cyn. Blvd.

Woodland Hills, CA 91303

ISBN 978-0-6151-8424-1

By Dottie Randazzo

Praying 101 for Spiritual Enlightenment

Praying 101 for Men

Praying 101 for Women

Praying 101 for Kids & Teens

Praying 101 for Parents

The Feeling

Trust

Are you a Spiritual Hypochondriac?

Gardening at Night

When the Soul Cries

Fiction

The Blue Girl

Someone asked me, "Shouldn't the title be '*How to **Leave** an Abusive Relationship*?'" If you have ever been in an abusive relationship you know you cannot LEAVE one. The only way out is to escape. An abusive relationship is like a prison; your every move is watched.

You don't have to be hit to be in an abusive relationship. Emotional abuse takes longer to heal from. Yes, bruises heal a lot faster.

If you have found yourself in an abusive relationship, the first thing you must do is stop beating yourself up for it. This isn't about you. If the abuser were not abusing you, they would be abusing someone else. Know that they have abused others in the past and will abuse others in the future. A sociopath is a person without a conscience. They are very dangerous people and they walk amongst us. Dr. Robert D. Hare reveals this chilling reality in his book, *Without Conscience: The Disturbing World of the Psychopaths Among Us.*

I know where you are and I know how you feel. I, too, found myself in an abusive relationship. I am sharing my story so you will know you aren't alone and I am sharing my escape plan to empower you to create your own escape plan. If I can do it, so can you.

Who am I? I am a smart, funny, successful woman. I was a smart, funny, successful woman when I found myself in an abusive relationship.

Trust your instincts. My ex-husband was introduced to me by mutual friends. He was 17 years older than I was. He was divorced and had grown children. Upon my first meeting with him, I felt compelled to ask him a question that I have never asked another human being. I asked him, "Have you ever hit an animal, child or old person?" Of course his answer was "No." He had not exhibited any behavior that would make me ask him this. Yet, something inside of me felt compelled to ask. I like to think that every time I ask a question, I will get a truthful answer.

I dated my ex-husband for two and a half years before moving in with him. The only violence I ever saw him exhibit was when he played ice hockey, which I didn't watch often. I never thought anything about it because everyone on the ice exhibited some sort of violence.

I moved in with him and we lived together for two and a half years before getting married. During the time we lived together, the only violence I witnessed was again, on the ice. I really thought I knew this man after five years.

We had a fairly large wedding. At my wedding a man I had never seen before came up to me and said "I have known your husband for 30 years. There is something you should know." He tried to get me alone, which was impossible; I was the bride. I forgot about the strange man at my wedding until one afternoon three months later when my phone rang. The man on the other end said, "Hi, my name is so-in-so and I tried to talk to you at your wedding." I instantly remembered who he was. He said, "You should know your husband used to beat his ex-wife." I was shocked. I asked, "What?" He said, "I just thought you should know," and hung up. I felt as if I was in a bad dream. I thought, *"What just happened?"*

I called my friends who introduced us and told them about the phone call. I asked, "What should I do?" My friends said that I was going to have to tell him about the phone call when he arrived home from work. I then decided to call my stepdaughter. She and I were close and I thought that she would tell me this guy who called me was whacked and I would feel better. I called her and told her about the phone call and asked her if it was true. She said, "Yes, but I think he has changed." I was shocked. I never, in a million years, thought that I would ever find myself in an abusive relationship with someone who hit people. That day, my life changed.

Upon his arrival home I told him about the phone call from the man. He tried to tell me not to believe strangers, that the caller was crazy, blah, blah, blah, but I interrupted him and told him I had called his daughter and she told me it was true. He put his head down, looking at the ground and said, "If I ever got that mad, I would leave, I would walk away." I know him saying this was supposed to make me feel better, but it didn't.

From that day forward, my husband was a different man than the one I knew prior to the phone call. The cat was out of the bag and there was no getting him back in it.

The next two and a half years were, by far, the worst years of my life. My husband began yelling and screaming at me all the time. We lived in California. I am originally from Louisiana. My nearest living relative was 2,300 miles away. As time went on, our relationship deteriorated. His yelling, slamming doors and throwing things escalated.

In 1995, we moved to Las Vegas. Now I was alone, no relatives and no friends. The abuse escalated. I never told one person what was happening in my home. Here are the reasons I never told anyone:

I was embarrassed and ashamed. I was an intelligent woman who began to wonder, *"How the hell did I get myself in this situation? This happens to other women, not me."*

I didn't think that they would believe me. My husband was O.J. Simpson charming. When he walked in a room, smiling and handsome, everyone thought he was the greatest. Little did they know that behind closed doors he was evil. I thought that everyone would think I was making it up to get out of my marriage.

I didn't want anyone to worry about me. I didn't want anyone constantly calling to see if I was okay because then he would get a clue that I had told someone the truth about him and it would make my situation worse.

I didn't want anyone else beating me up about how and why I got myself in this situation. It was bad enough that he was yelling at me and I was yelling at myself on the inside. I didn't need someone who had never been a situation like this to be on my back.

I beat myself up so badly about it that I began to have panic attacks. The mere sound of his car door would send me into a panic attack. I knew I would get yelled at for something, for anything. I had the feeling I couldn't even breathe right. You constantly live with a *damned if you do and damned if you don't* feeling.

A simple trip to the grocery store would send me into a panic and end badly. One evening, he said he wanted halibut for dinner. I went to the store and they didn't have halibut. I knew if I bought salmon I would get yelled at. I knew if I went home with no fish, I would get yelled at. It was a no-win situation.

The first time I saw him throw food was when I went to a fast food restaurant to pick up lunch and forgot to pick up butter for his corn. He was so outraged he threw the entire meal at the wall, all the time yelling and screaming about how stupid I was.

I tried a new recipe one evening and upon placing his plate in front of him, he took one look at it and hurled the plate to the wall as he began to yell and scream.

Another time I put his plate down and he asked, "Where are the salt and pepper shakers?" I was standing four feet from the table and reached to grab them from the counter while explaining that I had moved them to put a clean tablecloth on the table. Before I could get the salt and pepper shakers to the table, he had slammed his fist down, hurled his plate to the wall and yelled, "Only a stupid fucking idiot would forget to put the salt and pepper shaker back on the table."

I am proud to say, I never ever cleaned up the mess he made when he threw his food. I merely kept quiet and walked away.

There were many other things that occurred. It isn't important to mention them. These incidents were mentioned so that you would get the picture. Keep in mind, no one knew a thing of these incidents. All of this occurred at approximately the same time O.J. Simpson killed his wife. The world was sensitive to spousal abuse and I was thankful for it.

My husband was a big man, 6'2" tall and approximately 280 pounds. He was no match to my 5'6", 130 pounds. I am also proud to say he never hit me. I do not consider myself a wimp; however, I knew that when he was yelling and screaming at me, if I yelled back it would be like pouring fuel on the fire. I had knowledge that this man had crossed the line and hit before and there was nothing that would stop him from crossing the line again. I also knew that if anyone hits me, I will hit back and that they would have to kill me before I would stop defending myself. I knew, without a shadow of a doubt, that my life could end in a very tragic way.

I hated my life, all the while wondering, *"How the hell did this happen to me?"* I prayed every night that God would let him have a heart attack while he was playing hockey. I begged God to make him die, to please just take him. I had dreams of killing him. I always called my sister in my dreams, asking her to come and help me dig a hole or cut him up. I would look at the big bottle of Tylenol PM and think about how easy it would be to take the entire bottle. It was a thought that crossed my mind every single night.

I had to get away. I still did not want to tell anyone what was going on. I thought they would think I was stupid.

My birthday was approaching and I told my husband that instead of clothes or jewelry, I wanted a divorce as my present. He said he would never give me a divorce and he would break my arms and legs if I ever tried to leave him.

I had to make a plan to leave. Our lives were so intertwined. I had to make sure that once I left, he would never ever have an excuse to see me. I began slowly, by doing something every day that pertained to my escape. I also began to walk every day for several reasons.

I had gained a lot of weight during this time, eating all of the comfort foods. My favorite comfort food was Hagen Das® vanilla ice cream with cherries in it. It reminded me of the ice cream my dad used to make when I was five years old. When I ate it, I got that warm, loving feeling again, thinking of my dad. I ate a 2,000-calorie pint of this ice cream every day. I didn't know what emotional eating was until years later; I was sitting in the airport and my sister gave me that ice cream. The desire to eat it was gone. I looked at it and thanked her, but told her I no longer needed to eat it. It was then that I realized what a connection I had with that ice cream.

I also began walking for another reason. I needed to remove myself from my environment so I could think clearly. The walls and furniture in my home were the witnesses to my dilemma. I also was afraid that if I thought of leaving while in my home, my behavior might change and he would know and my situation would get uglier. So while walking every day, I thought about the life I wanted to live and I thought about the things I needed to do to get there.

I rented a storage unit and slowly began to pack up and move things there. I moved things that he would not notice were missing from the house. Every day, when I would move a box, my throat would begin to hurt. From the moment I hit the front door with the box until I was back home, my throat hurt. It was during that time I was the most fearful of getting caught.

I began pulling my information off of his computer when he was at work. I took all of our pictures and had duplicate copies of them made. I contacted the auto insurance company and explained that I was involved in a violent domestic situation and that I needed to have my own auto insurance without him on it and requested that I be taken off of his. Everyone I dealt with regarding my escape knew of the danger I would be in if they contacted him. I am forever thankful to everyone for their assistance and understanding.

I contacted a lawyer and began making payments for my divorce. Everything was in place so that once I had left, I could make the call and he would be served.

I decided I would leave in January 1997. The beginning of December 1996, my sister, brother-in-law and friend came to visit me in Las Vegas. One evening, we all decided to go out to dinner and then hit the Vegas strip. I asked my husband to join us. He informed us that he had a hockey game. The four of us proceeded to dinner and the strip. At 10:30pm, my husband called me and asked me where we were and what we were doing. I told him we were standing in front of the Treasure Island Hotel waiting for the Pirate show to begin and we would be home shortly. We arrived home at 1am. When I got into bed, he didn't say a word. He kept tossing and turning and huffing and puffing. At 5am I asked him if he was okay, thinking he might have heartburn or indigestion. He jumped up and yelled at the top of his lungs, "Okay, okay, no I am not okay." I asked him to keep his voice down or he would wake up everyone else. He slammed the bedroom door and yelled at the top of his lungs, "Fuck your sister, fuck her husband, fuck your friend and fuck you." He then proceeded to walk into the bathroom. I immediately put my robe on and walked into the living room. There was my friend, all dressed with suitcase in hand saying, "Take me to the airport. I am scared." My sister was standing there shocked. I, too, was shocked and embarrassed. This was the first time anyone was aware of the mad man I was living with. I tried to calm them down. He came out of the bedroom dressed and said, "Good Morning" to everyone like nothing had happened. Now my family was aware of my life.

My sister and brother-in-law said I couldn't stay there. I told them I had it under control and I had plans to leave in January. My sister begged me to leave sooner. My reason for staying until January was because approximately twenty of my husband's relatives were coming for the holidays. If I wasn't there, I felt that I would be ruining approximately twenty people's Christmas.

Ironically, my husband was being sued in California because he hit someone in the grocery store. He said that the guy took his grocery cart when his back was turned. His arbitration was scheduled for Monday, December 23^{rs}. My friend, who was in Las Vegas and witnessed the incident, is a lawyer. I asked him if he would tell my husband that he could assist him with his case by talking to him on Friday, December 20th. My husband decided he would drive to Los Angeles on Thursday, December 19th around 3pm after he had finished work. He would then be in Los Angeles with my friend the lawyer and there was my window to escape.

I planned to move in with my parents in Louisiana. I knew if I moved anywhere in Nevada or California, he would surely come after me. I knew that the distance and my dad would keep him from coming after me. My dad was alive at the time and I knew he would not let anyone hurt me.

In the weeks before December 20th, I sent my sister and cousin airline tickets to arrive in Las Vegas at 1pm on December 19th. I arranged for a U-Haul truck to be ready for pick up on December 19th. I arranged for movers to arrive on December 20th to help load the heavy furniture.

I picked up my sister and cousin at the airport at approximately 1pm. I gave them a beeper and dropped them off at a casino. When I beeped them, they would come to the front of the hotel and I would pick them up. They would be expecting me to beep them sometime between 3:30 and 4:30pm. My plan was to wait 30 minutes after he left before beeping them, just in case he had forgotten something and turned around to come back home.

Upon arriving home that day, my husband piddled and paddled around the house and did not leave when I thought he would. Around 5pm, he told me we were going to a casino for dinner. Upon arriving at the casino restaurant, we were informed that they could only serve cold sandwiches because a gas line had been broken. My husband became outraged and began yelling at me that I should have known about a gas line that was broken. I informed him we rented an all-electric home and didn't know why he thought I should know this. That was the last time he got to yell at me.

At 7:30pm on December 19, 1996, I said "Goodbye, drive safely." That would be the last time he ever laid eyes on me. For five years after that day, I said a daily prayer, "Dear God, please don't let this man ever, ever see me again. Please don't let this man ever lay an eye on me again. He is undeserving."

He drove away and I waited my self-imposed 30 minutes. I knew my sister and cousin were worried sick because they had not heard from me earlier as planned. I beeped them and picked them up at the casino. We immediately drove to pick up the truck. We spent the entire rest of the night packing. The next morning the moving men showed up to help us load the truck. While we were loading the truck, my husband began calling. I did not answer the phone. The more I let it ring, the angrier he became. My friend, the lawyer, who was with my husband while he was trying to get in touch with me, saw my husband get angry. He was scared.

At 1pm on December 20th, I dropped my cousin off at the airport as my sister and I drove away in my car and the U-Haul. We were exhausted. However, I did not want us to stop to rest until we were in another state. Somehow this made me feel safer. I called my mother to let her know we were safe and on the road. I didn't tell her where we were. I knew he would be calling her and I didn't want to put her in a position to lie. He did call her and she told him that I had left and she didn't know where I was.

On January 1st, 1997, my husband was served with divorce papers. I do believe that knowing I was surrounded by family deterred him from coming after me.

What I haven't told you is that I also moved my business at the same time.

I am a firm believer that every woman is a super woman and all you need is a plan.

You must do something that gets you out of your home every day so that you can think clearly. Take a walk, go to the gym or you can just sit in the dressing room at Target. It doesn't matter where you go.

Think about all the ways that your life is intertwined.

I am only going to suggest that you write things down if you have a safe place to bury your notebook. I would not want you to leave it in your car or your home or anyplace where it can be found.

Make a mental list of everything that you have in your life right now. Your clothes, your job, your furniture, your children, and anything else that you consider part of your life.

Now I want you to look at this list and pick out the things that cannot be replaced. You can replace your clothes, you can replace your job, you can replace your furniture and you can replace your home. You cannot replace your children and you cannot replace your face or life.

The things that you cannot replace should be the things that you value the most. This is what you should plan to leave with; if you are able to leave with clothes and furniture, then kudos to you. I took with me only furniture that I owned before we were married. I personally didn't want anything that we purchased together.

I want you to remember that you can do this. Just because you find yourself in this situation in which you feel like you have done the dumbest thing in your life…. does not mean you are stupid.

In leaving your current situation, you will not only be creating a better life for yourself, you will be empowering yourself in unimaginable ways.

When you find yourself alone, away from the situation and begin to think about leaving, ideas will flood your mind with ways to accomplish your goal.

I still am not a big fan of telling friends or relatives about the situation unless you are close to executing your escape or they can somehow assist you in your escape. The reasons are because you don't want to put someone in a position where they would have to lie or cover for you to protect you and also you wouldn't want someone to innocently say something and have something slip out that could cause the abuser to get more violent.

I also believe strongly in the power of prayer, even though God did not take my husband, and I prayed a million times that he would, I still believe. So pray, pray, pray. Pray for the wisdom to see and identify the things that you must do to plan your escape. Pray for the strength and courage to plan and execute your escape. Pray for your safety and the safety of others who have crossed paths with an abuser.

It is very important that you set a date that you will leave. Some day isn't on the calendar and not likely to happen. Once that you have set a date, you have made a mental commitment and everything will fall into place because your intent has been sealed.

You are going to need money to execute your escape. I was fortunate enough that I had my own income. You need cash, and if you are unemployed, you can get that cash by taking your jewelry to a pawnshop. You may and may not be able to get back your jewelry and valuables; however, things shouldn't be more important than your health and well-being. Pay for your lawyer, storage unit, truck rental, apartment deposit, rent, etc., with money orders. Money orders can be obtained at drug stores and post offices. Bury your receipts or throw them away. Do not bring anything into your home that is part of your escape plan.

I wish I could write out a more detailed plan of action for you to take. However, everyone's situation is different and I would not want you to follow a plan because it was written here; it may not be the plan for you.

Here are some helpful suggestions for you to consider when executing your own plan:

Stop beating yourself up for being in this situation. One person degrading you is enough. Be kind to yourself.

Make time every day away from your home to think about the life you want and your plan of escape.

Pray for wisdom, strength and courage.

Circle the date mentally when you will escape.

Evaluate what is truly valuable and worth taking and what isn't.

Find and put cash away to help
you escape.

Begin to do the things necessary for your escape.

Know that there are a lot of people who love you and want you to be safe and happy.

I am wishing you a safe escape
and wonderful love-filled life.

www.ingramcontent.com/pod-product-compliance
Lightning Source LLC
Chambersburg PA
CBHW032027040426
42448CB00006B/755